CARVED IN STONE

The Peter Watts Way of The Cross

Text by
Brother Paul Quenon

Photography by
Brother Patrick Hart

Ave Maria Press • Notre Dame, Indiana 46556

To the Memory of
THOMAS MERTON
1915-1968

© 1979 by Ave Maria Press, Notre Dame, Indiana 46556

All rights reserved. No part of this book may be reproduced or transmitted in any form or by any means, electronic or mechanical, including photocopying, recording, or by any information storage and retrieval system, without prior written permission from the publisher.

International Standard Book Number: 0-87793-195-X

Cover design: Joyce Stanley

Printed and bound in the United States of America.

CARVED IN STONE

Foreword

Today a number of paraliturgical practices and devotions are being revived, especially the recitation of the rosary and meditation on the way of the cross, which have for centuries nourished the lives of countless Christians. That thought inspired the publication of the following meditations with photographs of a contemporary set of the stations of the cross.

In the early 1950's a monk of Gethsemani discovered, quite by accident, a photograph of Peter Watts' stonework, and was so impressed with this English artist and disciple of Eric Gill, that Watts was commissioned (on the strength of that photograph) to execute a way of the cross in his native Bath stone. This was to be the first American commission for Mr. Watts, but not the last. Besides the statues of St. Benedict, St. Bernard, the Madonna and Child, the Sacred Heart and a large crucifix in Bath stone, which grace the cloisters at Gethsemani, Mr. Watts has since provided statues of singular beauty for many monastic communities as well as religious houses and parishes throughout the country.

For over two decades the monks of Gethsemani have lived with, and prayed before, the "Watts' Way of the Cross," but this is the first time to my knowledge that a monk has shared his personal experience of viewing the stations of the cross. To accompany his meditative texts, Brother Paul Quenon asked me to photograph the way of the cross, which I agreed to do, using the Canon FX camera that John Howard Griffin had loaned to Thomas Merton a decade earlier and which was returned to Gethsemani among the latter's personal effects, following his tragic death in Bangkok.

Brother Patrick Hart
Abbey of Gethsemani

JESUS ✝ IS CONDEMNED

I

Where is true authority?
Jesus who points to the source plainly bears it,
a regal presence who fills the square,
and already takes the first step that will
carry away all rule and ruin with him.

Power is too elusive and fickle.
Pilate will have nothing to do with it.
He doesn't want the right hand to see
what his left is doing.

And the servant boy —
neutrality between guilt and holiness —
he wonders if there is any bottom to the pitcher
or end to the stream of water
that will dissolve and carry away all misrule and tyranny
down through the ages.

II

Little crosses for little people
and big crosses for big people.

This is how we started out in the spiritual life.
And O how we clutched that child's-size cross to our ardent
 bosom!
But the cross outgrew us, and we became
entangled about it, inseparably,
like a vine around a tree.
Though upheld by it the vine must compete with
the tree for air,
and we wish that God's heavens were large enough
to let us stand untwisted and free
where there is no suffocation.

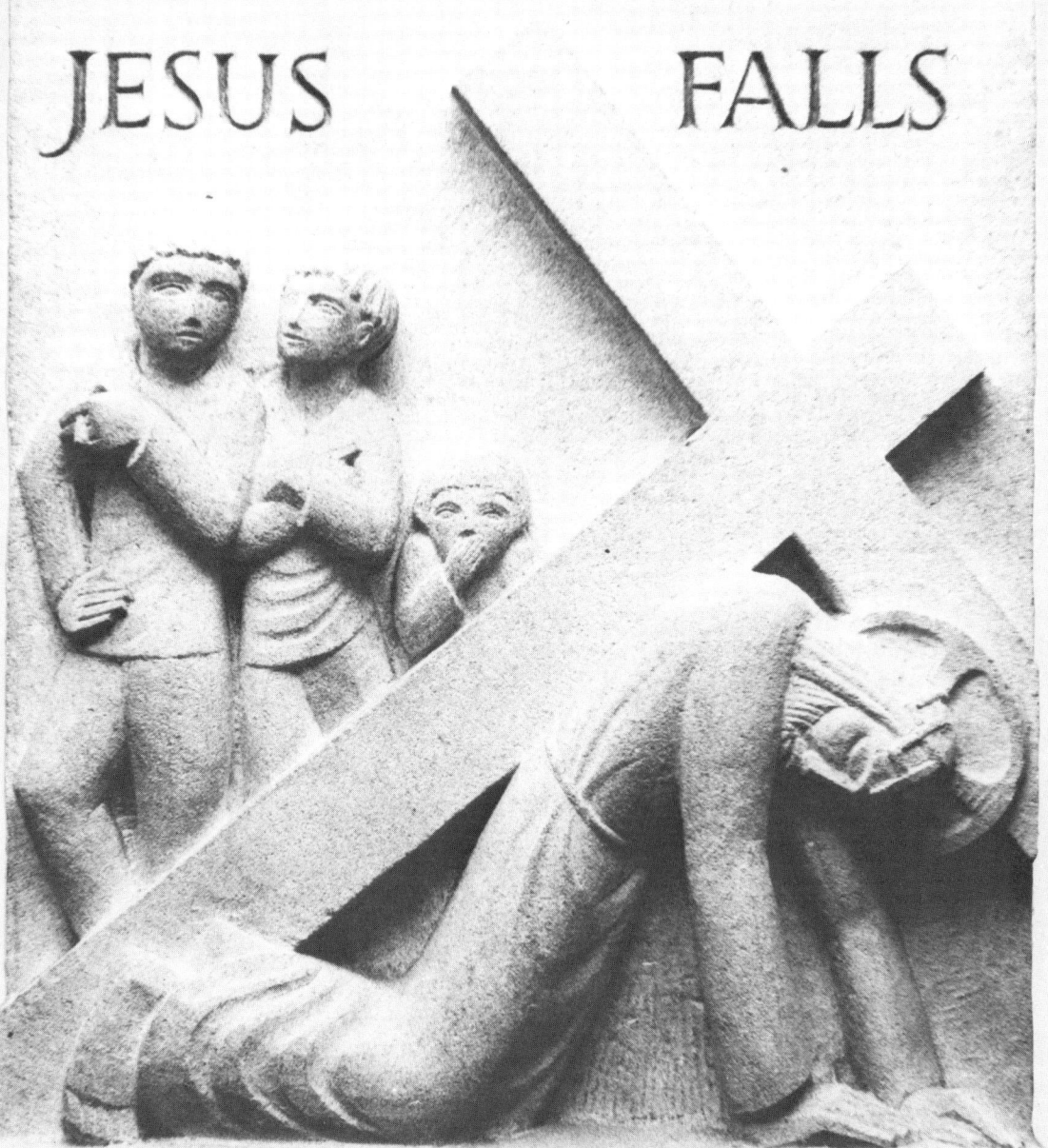

III

These were the early falls.
The first naughty giggle over a dirty word,
the first smoke, the swagger we could almost pull off,
the first time we snatched at a forbidden thing
and thought we had something to be guilty about—
failing to notice a man nearby
collapsed under a load.

Why should we notice?
He has always been there
like the everlasting hills around home.

We'll climb over the hill and see what is beyond.
There may be some even more enticing sight.

JESUS ✝ MEETS

HIS MOTHER

IV

Like reflecting mirrors, these two faces.

Jesus presses his countenance upon Mary.
His mother has impressed her image upon Jesus.

Jesus' arms encircle the cross and the mother
in one embrace, making inseparable the mother and
  the cross.
She gathers herself together and draws herself up
into his enveloping spirit,
where they both see without looking,
and mingle as two serene clouds,
turning darker, impenetrable

—we look away and pass onward.

SIMON

HELPS JESUS

V

At last, somebody strong has been found
to help the cross along,
but no one to help Jesus.

He leans against one sharp corner
like a drunkard about to slip off the bar stool.
And like a reluctant policeman
the big man hauls his load off the street,
but never looks at the derelict—
lest it arouse a smothered contempt.

Better to exist apart,
like strangers on different sides of the mountain.
Some are on the rise and some are in decline.
There's no vice in brushing elbows
as we pass a man on the way down
nor virtue in helping him get out of the way.

VI

She wanted no miracle.
To stand so close was too much discomfort,
and the removal of her veil
exposes hair like a solemn aureole
and her shy shoulders begging for covering.

A bit of his sweat was enough—
to wear forever on her head without,
but for her memory within—a word is impressed forever.

We see it pass between them.
All history knows that secret was spoken,
but only she knows what was said,
and is said even now.
We have enshrined and worshiped the outer veil, but have missed
what it covered within.

VII

Like a team of stallions
they come galloping onto the scene,
our middle years,
with zeal for truth, righteousness
and vengeance against the wrong—
which means whatever is already
down, helpless, and without defense.

If God has made such a failure of history
we will remake it on our own.
Our weapons will be the bricks on which we walk and
we will grind the kingdom
into the dust beneath our feet.
Let him try to reverse our course,
and raise up, if he will,
sons of Abraham from these stones.

VIII

They plead for their children
and pray for him to lift the sentence
against the fruit of their womb.
But he undercuts their prayer,
for so must destiny stand.
God has subjected all things to judgment.
And Jesus' awkward hand,
upturned in a difficult teaching,
is joined to the woman's strong breadloaf
to form the initial T:

for the Truth of what must come to pass?
or for the cross which joins them forever
in their inseparable suffering?

JESUS FALLS

A THIRD TIME

IX

"I am a worm and no man . . . the laughingstock
of the people."

We forgive ourselves once, twice,
but the third fall is worse than death.
It leaves us feeling like a wet noodle
and unable to face the gaze of other people.

Like a worm we would prefer to cling to the earth,
except that the cross pries us up,
and the one at the other end of the lever
is another sinner like ourself.

Maybe he has already seen his third fall,
his fourth or fifth. . . .

X

How modest, like nursemaids
in a nightly bedtime ritual,
who prepare this willowy youngster
for his restful sleep.

We will tuck him away and he will float off
to dreamland, and all will be quiet again
as it was before he became so
noisy, obnoxious and tiresome.
Such a Lamb he is now that we put him away!
It must be the right thing to do after all.
And it is for his best interest really.
We'll be in a much better mood when this is all over.

Meanwhile, don't look too closely
lest those naked tremblings unnerve us. . . .

XI

Strange how in the midst of the most constructive jobs
you are seized by a moment of anxiety—
like a doubt whether you turned off the stove at home.

And philosophers tell rumors that
at the core of creation is a spreading death.
We who build up the world
are thieves against death.
The world is comprised of the good thieves
and the bad thieves:
those who suspect what they are doing
and those who always ignore it.

Such doubts are aroused by
One who howls against the flat heavens,
whose contagious echo protests against
our pinning life down like a captured butterfly,
One whose thrashing limbs deny
our painless and insensible refusal to live.

JESUS DIES ON THE CROSS

XII

A cross was not found tall enough to hold him in death.
The vine grew and bore fruit, and outreached the tree.
His branches stretch out to fill the land
like the new heavens,
like the wings of the descending dove.

And underneath, vast empty space,
enough for multitudes,
too empty for the lone solitary there in distress.
For her the world is too big in life
as it is too small for him in death,

and we are drawn to fill her grief,
to raise a chorus of lamentation
unto the tranquil sun of that head
sinking toward death.

XIII

At last we can come close to him.
His size finally fits our measure.
We can hold him and be reconciled—
after all these years.
Death has set to him a limit.
There is no more struggle with divinity,
no more the grand absences and presences,
only our own image and likeness
as we know it for sure.

Recognition leads to acceptance,
and acceptance brings us to love.
Such is the lowly path for mortals.
Not until we feel it limp and cold beneath our touch
do we know the life that was taken
has been given,
and was always given, by God.

JESUS ✝

IS LAID IN THE TOMB

XIV

Like a basket of summer fruit
the harvest is brought home.

And we are devoted keepers of the generous store,
serving with flourishing ritual and copious chants
his brief stay.
For our whole life is but a three-day span.

Monks have the special art of preparing for burial,
which is preparation for life,
for our dwelling is Christ's place of burial
where we have died with him that we may live with him.

As he was our unwanted friend throughout life,
so we have become his constant companions in death,
that when the light breaks forth
and this present life falls away
we may be one with him in a resurrection of glory.